COREY S. SHANNON

LINKEDIN OPTIMIZATION 2024

How to Land your Dream Job with An Up-to-date Strategy to help Optimize your LinkedIn Profile and Build your Network

Copyright © 2024 by Corey S. Shannon

All rights reserved. No part of this publication may be reproduced, stored or transmitted in any form or by any means, electronic, mechanical, photocopying, recording, scanning, or otherwise without written permission from the publisher. It is illegal to copy this book, post it to a website, or distribute it by any other means without permission.

First edition

Cover art by PELUMI MAKINDE

This book was professionally typeset on Reedsy.
Find out more at reedsy.com

Contents

INTRODUCTION	iv
CHAPTER 1: THE POWER OF YOUR LINKEDIN PROFILE	1
Importance of LinkedIn in today's job market	2
Why a strong profile is crucial for landing your dream job	3
Benefits of an optimized LinkedIn profile	6
CHAPTER 2: BUILDING A FOUNDATION FOR SUCCESS	9
10 Strategies and Tips to Optimize your LinkedIn Profile	9
CHAPTER 3: BUILDING YOUR NETWORK: THE POWER OF CONNECTIONS	14
Be active on LinkedIn.	14
Connect with colleagues and past employers	14
Engage with Industry Leaders	17
Join Relevant Groups	19
CHAPTER 4: LANDING YOUR DREAM JOB	22
Advanced Search Filters: Targeting Your Ideal Job	22
Job Alerts: Staying Ahead of the Curve	23
The Perfect Pairing: Combining Search Filters and Job Alerts	24
The Power of "Easy Apply"	25
CHAPTER 5: MAINTAINING YOUR PRESENCE	26
Staying Active & Engaged (Art of Consistency)	26
Advanced Features for Power Users	27
BONUS CHAPTER - PRO TIPS & AVOIDING COMMON PITFALLS	28
Common Missteps to Steer Clear Of:	28
Advanced Profile Optimization Techniques:	29

INTRODUCTION

Is your LinkedIn profile a sleeping giant?

Imagine your dream job within reach, but potential employers can't find you online. **LinkedIn** is the modern goldmine for career seekers, but simply having a profile isn't enough. This book is your wake-up call, a roadmap to transforming your LinkedIn presence from a ghost town into a thriving professional hub that attracts opportunity.

Ready to unlock the power of LinkedIn and land your dream job? This comprehensive guide equips you with winning strategies to:

- Craft a profile that screams **expertise** and grabs recruiter attention.
- Master **advanced search filters and job alerts** to target your ideal position.
- Build a powerful **network** that opens doors to new opportunities.
- **Engage with industry leaders** and position yourself as a thought leader.
- Leverage the platform for **continuous learning and career development**.

Don't let your LinkedIn profile gather dust. This book is your key to unlocking its potential and propelling your career forward.

CHAPTER 1: THE POWER OF YOUR LINKEDIN PROFILE

LinkedIn boasts a staggering **740 million registered users** as of October 2023, making it the world's largest professional networking platform. More importantly, **over 95% of recruiters** actively search this platform to find talented individuals like you. This translates to millions of professionals actively searching for talent, making it a gold mine for job seekers like you.

Think of your LinkedIn profile as your digital storefront; it's the first impression you make on potential employers, recruiters, and industry leaders. A strong, well-maintained profile can be the key that unlocks a world of exciting career opportunities.

From Applicant to All-Star: A Real-Life Example

Let's face it, the traditional job search can feel frustrating. Take Sarah, for example. Stuck in a dead-end marketing role, she craved a more fulfilling career. But then, she discovered the magic of LinkedIn optimization. By revamping her profile with the strategies we'll explore in this book, Sarah transformed her online presence. Her profile, now loaded with relevant keywords and showcasing her accomplishments, started attracting the attention of top recruiters. Within a few months, she landed interviews at her dream companies and ultimately secured a fantastic marketing role at a leading agency. Sarah's story is a testament to how a strategic LinkedIn profile can open doors to exciting career possibilities.

Importance of LinkedIn in today's job market

Targeted Job Search and Increased Visibility

Unlike generic job boards, LinkedIn allows you to tailor your profile and search for opportunities that perfectly align with your skills and experience. By properly employing keywords and improving your profile, you can ensure that the appropriate hiring managers notice your qualifications.

Building Your Personal Brand and Establishing Expertise

LinkedIn serves as your online professional portfolio. You can showcase your accomplishments, skills, and experience, crafting a compelling narrative that highlights your value proposition. By sharing industry insights, engaging in discussions, and publishing content, you can establish yourself as a thought leader within your field, attracting potential employers seeking top talent.

A Platform for Continuous Learning and Development

LinkedIn Learning, a built-in feature, offers a vast library of online courses on various professional development topics. Completing these courses and showcasing them on your profile demonstrates your commitment to lifelong learning and staying ahead of the curve in your industry.

Boosting Your Credibility and Social Proof

Recommendations and endorsements from colleagues and past employers add credibility and social proof to your profile. This can significantly increase your appeal to potential employers, who can see firsthand your skills and work ethic through the positive feedback of others in your network.

Staying Connected and Informed

LinkedIn allows you to follow companies, industry leaders, and influencers. This keeps you updated on the latest job openings, industry trends, and professional insights, allowing you to make informed career decisions and stay competitive in your field.

Beyond Landing a Job: A Long-Term Career Tool

LinkedIn isn't just about landing your next job; it's a long-term career management tool. You can foster valuable connections, build relationships with potential mentors, and explore new opportunities as your career evolves.

Why a strong profile is crucial for landing your dream job

The job hunt can feel like navigating a crowded marketplace. Resumes fly under the radar, and opportunities seem to slip through your fingers. But what if there was a powerful tool at your disposal—a digital storefront that could showcase your skills and experience directly to potential employers? Enter LinkedIn, the professional networking platform that has revolutionized the way we approach our careers.

Here's why a strong LinkedIn profile is no longer optional for landing your dream job:

First Impressions Matter: Your Digital Handshake

Imagine walking into a job interview with a wrinkled shirt and a coffee stain on your resume. Not ideal, right? Your LinkedIn profile serves as your digital first impression. A well-crafted profile with a professional headshot and a compelling headline sets the tone and grabs the attention of recruiters and hiring managers.

Standing Out in a Sea of Applicants: The Power of Optimization

The job market is competitive, and recruiters often wade through hundreds of resumes. An optimized LinkedIn profile acts as a beacon, attracting attention with relevant keywords.

Beyond the Resume: Telling Your Story with Impact

Your LinkedIn profile goes beyond simply listing past jobs. It's a platform to tell your professional story in a dynamic and engaging way. Use strong action verbs and quantifiable achievements to showcase the impact you've made in previous roles. Don't just say you were "responsible for"; demonstrate how you "spearheaded," "managed," or "developed."

Establishing Authority and Expertise: More Than Just Qualifications

A strong LinkedIn profile goes beyond listing your skills. It's a platform to establish yourself as an expert in your field. Share industry insights, engage in relevant discussions, and consider publishing articles or blog posts to demonstrate your knowledge and passion. This positions you as a thought leader and attracts potential employers seeking top talent.

Building Your Network: The Power of Connections

LinkedIn is a powerful networking tool. It allows you to connect with past colleagues, mentors, and industry influencers. By strategically building your network, you open doors to new opportunities, gain valuable career advice, and potentially land referrals for your dream job.

A Showcase for Continuous Learning:

Never stop learning! LinkedIn Learning offers a vast library of online courses on various professional development topics. Completing these courses and adding them to your profile demonstrates your commitment to lifelong learning and staying relevant in your field.

The Key Takeaway: Invest in Yourself

Crafting a strong LinkedIn profile requires time and effort, but it's an investment in your career future. By leveraging the platform's features and showcasing your skills and experience, you increase your visibility, establish yourself as an expert, and ultimately unlock a world of possibilities, bringing you one step closer to landing your dream job.

Benefits of an optimized LinkedIn profile

In today's digital age, your online presence plays a critical role in your career success. Among professional platforms, LinkedIn reigns supreme. But simply having a profile isn't enough. To truly stand out and attract opportunities, you need an optimized profile that showcases your value and grabs the attention of recruiters and hiring managers.

Here's how a well-crafted LinkedIn profile can unlock a world of career benefits:

Enhanced visibility and searchability:

An optimized profile is like a beacon in the vast online landscape. By strategically incorporating relevant keywords throughout your profile, from your headline to your experience section, you increase your chances of appearing in recruiter searches. This ensures that your qualifications are discovered by the right people at the right time.

Credibility and Social Proof:

A well-maintained profile with a compelling narrative demonstrates professionalism and dedication. Including quantifiable achievements, positive recommendations from colleagues, and relevant skills with endorsements adds credibility to your profile and gives employers confidence in your abilities.

CHAPTER 1: THE POWER OF YOUR LINKEDIN PROFILE

Establishing Yourself as an Expert:

LinkedIn is more than just a digital resume; it's a platform to showcase your expertise. Sharing industry insights, engaging in discussions, and publishing articles allows you to position yourself as a thought leader. This not only attracts potential employers seeking top talent but also expands your network and establishes valuable professional connections.

Targeted networking and stronger connections:

LinkedIn allows you to connect with professionals across your industry, from past colleagues and mentors to potential collaborators and hiring managers. By strategically building your network, you open doors to new opportunities, gain valuable insights, and potentially land referrals for your dream job.

A Platform for Continuous Learning and Development:

Never stop learning! LinkedIn Learning offers a treasure trove of online courses on various professional development topics. Completing these courses and adding them to your profile demonstrates your commitment to continuous learning and staying relevant in your field.

Increased Interview Invitations and Improved Job Prospects:

An optimized profile acts as a powerful marketing tool for your skills and experience. By highlighting your accomplishments and showcasing your value proposition, you're more likely to receive interview invitations and land your dream job.

Career Management Tool Beyond Job Hunting:

LinkedIn offers benefits beyond just landing your next job. It's a platform for long-term career management. You can stay updated on industry trends, connect with potential mentors, and explore new opportunities as your career evolves.

CHAPTER 2: BUILDING A FOUNDATION FOR SUCCESS

Imagine walking into a job interview with a wrinkled shirt and a coffee stain on your resume. Not ideal, right? Your LinkedIn profile deserves the same level of care and attention. Just like a polished resume, a strong LinkedIn profile is built on a solid foundation. This chapter guides you through the essential steps to create a professional and optimized profile that will grab the attention of recruiters and hiring managers.

10 Strategies and Tips to Optimize your LinkedIn Profile

1. Crafting Your Digital Persona: Profile Picture

First impressions matter, and your profile picture is your digital handshake. Opt for a professional headshot that showcases your personality. A friendly smile and a clean background go a long way.

Get a photographer, or just use your iPhone to take a great shot. The idea is to create a picture that is honest, professional, warm, inviting, pleasant, and confident. That is what you want to express.

Avoid photographs that are imprecise or that make it difficult for recruiters to recognize you. A good example would be group or couple photographs. These don't come across as professional. Other sorts of images to avoid are those in which you are not staring at the camera or ones that resemble your graduation shot from years ago. Avoid wearing sunglasses in your profile photo.

Lastly, avoid AI photos; LinkedIn or other users might think you are a bot. A professional profile photo increases your chances of being noticed and receiving opportunities by 12 times or more.

2. Have a custom background image.

I believe this is underutilized. Many individuals are aware of this, but they do not make full use of it. You may change your picture to anything you like. You might use your initials, your value proposition statement, contact information, or a link to your website. To stand out, you should employ something original and unusual.

3. Create an appealing, essential, and optimized headline.

Your title is the first thing visitors and recruiters see as they scroll through the search results; therefore, you want to create a headline that grabs their attention. This is because if you don't change it, it will be your most recent employment title.

To maximize your headline, begin by incorporating the title you're aiming for. Second, choose terms that are relevant to your location. The third component is your value proposition statement, also known as an impact statement, which will help people comprehend your distinct differentiator. Make it entertaining, and stress the points you believe are significant.

Now, keep in mind that there is a character restriction, but there is a method around it. This is to change your headline on the LinkedIn mobile app, which presently has no character restriction.

4. Create an authentic and optimized about summary.

This is what I refer to as the ultimate space, where you may write anything to capture the reader's attention. Most people either do not write anything or write only a few sentences. This is a disadvantage for them because you may add a variety of items to your summary.

My advice is to tell a paragraph about yourself, your passions, and what you care about. Next, list your top three unique selling features, or core area knowledge or abilities. From there, elaborate further and explain what it means. Share certain stories or instances.

Finally, use bullet points to highlight your core areas of expertise. Put in some relevant keywords. So this will assist you with your search rankings. Finally, you may invite others to connect with you and share your contact information. Thus, if you want to stand out, you must provide some context for what you do and what you've done thus far.

5. Do not forget to optimize your job titles.

This may appear to be a straightforward concept, yet job titles can vary among sectors and firms. If your work title is not popular, you may wish to include a bracket or another job title that is equal. For example, I recently discovered someone's profile as a client success coach. It is comparable to the roles of client success manager and account manager. You should bracket such job titles to improve your exposure and search rankings.

6. Ensure that the Experience Information section is optimized

This is also a free place where you can expound on your abilities. I propose writing a paragraph and publishing three lines max that describe the broad scope of your job. This includes your primary work tasks and obligations. To stand out, provide three to five bullet points with your essential highlights. This might include your primary successes and noteworthy results from how you contributed value to your firm. If you can think of actual outcomes to discuss, it will also help you get people's attention.

7. Optimize your skills section for better search rankings.

You can include up to 50 skill sets in your profile. LinkedIn also lets you pin at least three talents. So these are the main ones you want to emphasize, together with the appropriate keywords. My advice is to determine the functional critical abilities, or hard skills, that recruiters are looking for. Avoid soft skills. Product Management, User Experience, and Data Analysis are some of the most important functional skills for a Product Manager.

8. Have strong endorsements and recommendations.

This is in reference to your talent area in your skill section. What fundamental talents do you want to be recognized and recommended for? That is why it is important to obtain at least three to five references from previous colleagues, your employer, and those who deal with you, your clients, and so on. You need such testimonials since they will help you gain credibility and be perceived as a top performer with great potential.

9. Write articles to share your expertise.

This is the place where you may share your narrative, ideas, major trends, opportunities, and difficulties in the field you work in. This gives the appearance that you have tremendous knowledge and competence in your area. You can write three to five articles. That's already an excellent start. It will give them an impression of your communication skills, writing skills, and critical thinking abilities, all of which are important when determining if someone is qualified to be a candidate.

10. Take advantage of the feature section.

This one is relatively new, and few people are aware of it. It may be found directly below the Summary section. This is an excellent opportunity to stand out because it provides several possibilities for you. For example, you might include a link to a video introducing yourself or to previous posts or articles you've published on LinkedIn. Perhaps you might mention accolades, credentials, or your portfolio. This is a creative method to make your online CV stand out.

CHAPTER 3: BUILDING YOUR NETWORK: THE POWER OF CONNECTIONS

LinkedIn is a powerful networking tool. Here are some ways to expand your network and increase your visibility.

Be active on LinkedIn.

Building your network starts with thorough activeness on LinkedIn, which is a powerful tool for making connections. Here,s why:

After you've completed and optimized your profile, be sure to stay active on LinkedIn to improve your marketability, searchability, and exposure. Every time you click a like, comment, or share, it is featured or exhibited in your network feed. This will put you at the forefront of people's minds in your network. This will open up a lot of chances for you, which will be beneficial.

Connect with colleagues and past employers

The professional world thrives on connections. In today's digital age, LinkedIn offers an invaluable platform to reconnect with colleagues and past employers, fostering valuable relationships that can benefit your career in unexpected ways.

Here are some strategies to navigate reconnecting on LinkedIn:

1. The Art of Reconnecting: Striking the Right Balance

Remember, time has passed. Before sending a connection request, consider the nature of your relationship with the person. For close colleagues or recent employers, a personalized message is a thoughtful touch. Briefly reintroduce yourself, mention a specific memory you share (if appropriate), and express your desire to reconnect.

2. Keep it Short and Sweet: Making a Positive First Impression

When crafting your connection request message, be concise and professional. A sentence or two reminding them who you are and expressing your interest in reconnecting is sufficient. Avoid lengthy messages or personal details that might not be relevant in a professional setting.

3. Highlight Common Ground: Emphasize Mutual Benefits

People are more likely to connect when they see a potential benefit. Briefly mention something you've learned from them, a shared industry interest, or an update on your career path. Show them how reconnecting with you could be mutually beneficial.

4. Respect Their Time and Boundaries:

Not everyone might be comfortable reconnecting online. If your request goes unanswered, don't take it personally. There could be various reasons, and a follow-up message after a reasonable amount of time (like a few weeks) is acceptable. However, be respectful of their decision and avoid being overly persistent.

5. Turning Connections into Opportunities

Once you've reconnected, nurture the relationship. Like and comment on their relevant posts, share industry insights they might find valuable, or offer congratulations on their achievements. This keeps you on their radar and fosters trust.

6. The Power of Information: Staying Updated

Pay attention to their updates. Are they hiring for new positions at their company? Do they share articles relevant to your career goals? This information can be invaluable when seeking new opportunities or exploring career shifts.

7. Beyond Networking: Building Meaningful Relationships

While reconnecting can lead to career benefits, remember the importance of genuine connections. Offer support, celebrate their successes, and be someone they can rely on as well. Building strong professional relationships goes a long way in today's dynamic job market.

Engage with Industry Leaders

To level up your network, one powerful way to go about it is by engaging with industry leaders on LinkedIn. These influential figures can offer valuable insights, inspire your career path, and even open doors to new opportunities. Here's how to strategically connect and engage with industry leaders on this key professional platform:

1. Identify Your Leaders: Following the Right People

The first step is to identify the industry leaders you want to connect with. Consider their area of expertise, their leadership style, and the value they can bring to your professional development. Utilize LinkedIn's search function and filter by industry, job title, or company to find relevant profiles.

2. Follow and Observe: Learning from the Best

Start by following these industry leaders. Pay attention to the content they share, the discussions they participate in, and the groups they engage with. This allows you to glean valuable insights into their perspective on industry trends, challenges, and opportunities.

3. Add Value to the Conversation: Insightful Participation

Don't just lurk! Aim to participate in discussions where industry leaders are present. Share thoughtful comments, ask insightful questions related to their posts, and offer your own unique perspective on relevant topics. This demonstrates your knowledge and establishes you as a valuable contributor to the conversation.

4. Connect Strategically: Respectful Approaches

Once you've established a presence by engaging with their content, consider sending a connection request. Keep it concise and professional. Briefly introduce yourself, mention why you admire their work, and highlight a specific post or discussion that resonated with you.

5. Beyond the Request: Building Long-Term Connections

The goal isn't just a connection; it's fostering a relationship. Continue to engage with their content, offering congratulations on achievements or sharing relevant articles they might find interesting. This demonstrates your genuine interest and builds trust over time.

6. Leverage Opportunities: Learning from Interactions

Industry leaders often host live Q&A sessions or participate in group discussions. Actively participate in these events! Ask thoughtful questions, showcase your knowledge, and learn from their expertise. This direct interaction can leave a lasting impression and potentially open doors for future mentorship or collaboration.

7. The Power of Community: Participating in Industry Groups

Many industry leaders participate in relevant LinkedIn groups. Join these groups and actively participate in discussions. This positions you alongside thought leaders and allows you to network with a wider range of professionals within your field.

Remember, It's a Marathon, Not a Sprint

Building relationships with industry leaders takes time and effort. Be patient, consistent, and offer genuine value.

Join Relevant Groups

LinkedIn groups are a fantastic way to connect with like-minded professionals. Join groups in your industry and actively participate in discussions.

1. Expand your network and make meaningful connections

Groups connect you with like-minded professionals in your industry, alumni from your alma mater, or individuals with shared interests. This allows you to build valuable relationships beyond your immediate connections, fostering a sense of belonging and opening doors to potential collaborations or future opportunities.

2. Stay current on industry trends and insights

Groups often serve as a breeding ground for industry news, discussions, and expert opinions. Actively participating allows you to stay informed about the latest trends, challenges, and advancements within your field. This keeps your knowledge base sharp and positions you as someone who's engaged and passionate about your industry.

3. Showcase your expertise and build credibility

Groups provide a platform for you to share your own insights and expertise. By participating in discussions, answering questions thoughtfully, and offering valuable contributions, you establish yourself as a thought leader within your niche. This not only builds your credibility but also increases your visibility to potential employers or collaborators.

4. Find mentors and learn from industry leaders.

Many groups feature established professionals and industry leaders. Observe their interactions, learn from their experiences, and don't hesitate to ask insightful questions. This exposure to valuable mentorship can significantly accelerate your professional growth.

5. Discover new career opportunities (discreetly):

Groups can be a treasure trove for hidden job opportunities. Companies sometimes post job openings within relevant groups, or members might share leads on interesting positions. Keep your eyes peeled (but avoid overt job-hunting behavior); you never know what valuable connections might lead to your dream job.

6. Strengthen your communication and networking skills.

Active participation in group discussions hones your communication skills. You learn to articulate your ideas clearly, engage in respectful debates, and network effectively with a diverse range of professionals. These refined communication skills can significantly enhance your overall professional presence.

Finding the Perfect Fit: How to Choose Relevant Groups

- **Industry Focus:** Prioritize groups specific to your industry or area of expertise.
- **Location Focus:** Consider joining groups with a regional focus to connect with local professionals.
- **Skill-Based Focus:** Explore groups dedicated to specific skills you want to develop.
- **Company-Affiliated Groups:** If interested in a particular company, joining their LinkedIn group can be a strategic move.

Engaging Effectively: How to Make the Most of Groups

- **Be an active participant;** don't just lurk! Share your insights, answer questions, and contribute to discussions.
- **Respectful Communication:** Maintain a professional tone, avoid negativity, and contribute meaningfully to the conversation.
- **Post Valuable Content:** Share industry articles, pose insightful questions, and offer helpful resources to the group.
- **Network Strategically:** Connect with interesting individuals, participate in private messages if appropriate, and build long-term professional relationships.

CHAPTER 4: LANDING YOUR DREAM JOB

Your profile is polished, you're showcasing your expertise, and your network is growing fantastically! Now, let's leverage LinkedIn's powerful tools to land your dream job.

LinkedIn boasts robust job alerts and a search engine designed to connect you with the perfect opportunity. Here's how to use it effectively:

Advanced Search Filters: Targeting Your Ideal Job

Imagine a job board that displays only the positions that perfectly align with your skills and experience. Advanced Search Filters on LinkedIn make this a reality. Here's how to unlock their potential:

- **Location, Location, Location:** Specify your desired work location, whether it's a specific city, state, or remote opportunities.
- **Industry Matters:** Target your search by industry to ensure you're only seeing relevant job postings.
- **Experience matters too:** Filter by years of experience to match your qualifications with the requirements.
- **Keywords are Key:** Strategically incorporate keywords from your resume

and desired job titles to pinpoint the most relevant openings.
- **Company Culture Counts:** Refine your search by company size, culture, or specific employers you're interested in.
- **Job Type Matters:** Choose between full-time, part-time, contract, or freelance positions to find the work arrangement that best suits your needs.

Pro Tip: Don't be afraid to combine multiple filters! The more specific you are, the higher your chances of finding your dream job.

Job Alerts: Staying Ahead of the Curve

Finding the perfect job often requires timing. Job Alerts ensure you don't miss out on new opportunities that match your criteria. Here's how to set them up for success:

- **Customize Your Alerts:** Mirroring your Advanced Search Filter criteria, create personalized job alerts that target your ideal positions.
- **Frequency is key.** Set the alert frequency to receive notifications daily, weekly, or at a pace that suits your job search timeframe.
- **Stay Informed, Stay Ahead:** Job Alerts deliver new opportunities directly to your inbox, ensuring you're always aware of the latest relevant openings.
- **Manage Your Alerts:** As your job search progresses, you can easily edit or delete your existing alerts to reflect your evolving needs.

The Perfect Pairing: Combining Search Filters and Job Alerts

For a truly powerful job search strategy, combine Advanced Search Filters with Job Alerts. By filtering your search and setting up alerts for specific criteria, you create an automated system that delivers the most relevant opportunities directly to you. This saves you time and ensures you're at the forefront of the competition for your dream job.

Tailoring Your Profile for Every Application

It's tempting to use a generic profile for every job application. However, taking the time to tailor your profile to each specific role can significantly increase your chances of landing an interview. Here's how:

- **Keyword Optimization:** Carefully review the job description and strategically weave relevant keywords throughout your profile. This increases your visibility to recruiters searching for candidates with those specific skills.
- **Highlight Relevant Achievements:** Showcase accomplishments from your experience that directly relate to the job requirements. Remember, quantifiable results always make a strong impression.
- **Customize Your Summary:** Tailor your profile summary to emphasize the skills and experience most relevant to the specific position.

The Power of "Easy Apply"

LinkedIn's "Easy Apply" feature allows you to submit applications directly through the platform. While it's convenient, remember that it's not a substitute for a personalized cover letter.

Pro Tip: Consider including a brief cover letter within the application itself, highlighting your key qualifications and enthusiasm for the opportunity.

Leveraging Your Network

Remember, your network is a valuable asset in your job search.

- **Informational Interviews:** Reach out to individuals in your network who work at your target companies. Schedule informational interviews to learn more about the company's culture and potential roles.
- **Employee Referrals:** Don't underestimate the power of referrals! Let your network know you're on the job hunt and inquire about potential referral opportunities.

CHAPTER 5: MAINTAINING YOUR PRESENCE

Congratulations! You've optimized your profile, landed interviews, and hopefully secured your dream job. But your work on LinkedIn doesn't stop there. Here's how to maintain a thriving online presence and explore advanced features to stay competitive.

Staying Active & Engaged (Art of Consistency)

Just like a well-maintained garden, your LinkedIn profile needs consistent care to flourish. Here are some ways to keep your profile active and engaging:

- **Regular Updates:** Regularly update your profile with new achievements, skills, or certifications. This demonstrates your ongoing professional development and keeps your profile fresh for recruiters.
- **Engage with Content:** Don't just post; actively engage with content from others. Like, comment, and share thought-provoking articles or discussions to stay visible and build relationships.
- **Participate in Industry Discussions:** Continue participating in relevant group discussions and answering questions thoughtfully. This positions you as an expert and allows you to connect with potential collaborators or future employers.

Advanced Features for Power Users

LinkedIn offers a variety of advanced features to take your profile and network to the next level:

- **LinkedIn Learning:** This platform offers a vast library of online courses on various professional development topics. Completing courses and showcasing them on your profile demonstrates your commitment to continuous learning.
- **LinkedIn Sales Navigator (for Sales Professionals):** This premium feature offers advanced search filters and lead generation tools specifically designed for sales professionals.
- **LinkedIn Recruiter (for Recruiters):** This premium service allows recruiters to source candidates and manage their talent pipelines more efficiently.

BONUS CHAPTER - PRO TIPS & AVOIDING COMMON PITFALLS

Throughout this book, we've explored strategies to craft a compelling LinkedIn profile that gets noticed. In this bonus chapter, we'll delve into some common mistakes to avoid and explore advanced techniques to take your profile optimization to the next level.

Common Missteps to Steer Clear Of:

- **Incompleteness:** An incomplete profile creates a negative impression. Ensure all relevant sections are filled out with accurate and up-to-date information.
- **Generic Profile:** Avoid a generic profile that could apply to anyone. Tailor your profile to showcase your unique skills and experience.
- **Grammar and typos:** proofread your profile meticulously! Typos and grammatical errors come across as unprofessional.
- **Inactivity:** A dormant profile gets lost in the sea of active users. Regularly update your profile and engage with content to maintain visibility.
- **Overselling Yourself:** Confidence is great, but avoid overstating your qualifications or embellishing your accomplishments. Focus on honesty and authenticity.

BONUS CHAPTER - PRO TIPS & AVOIDING COMMON PITFALLS

Advanced Profile Optimization Techniques:

- **Customizing your URL:** A generic URL with a string of numbers looks impersonal. Claim your custom URL with your name for a professional touch.
- **Adding a Background Image:** A visually appealing background image can enhance your profile's aesthetics. Choose an image that aligns with your brand and industry.
- **Publishing Long-Form Content:** While short snippets are valuable, consider publishing longer-form content like articles to establish yourself as a thought leader.
- **Joining LinkedIn Live Events:** Participating in live events hosted by industry influencers can boost your visibility and allow you to connect with a wider audience.
- **Engaging with Polls and Surveys:** LinkedIn polls and surveys offer a fun way to engage with your network and demonstrate your industry knowledge.

www.ingramcontent.com/pod-product-compliance
Lightning Source LLC
Chambersburg PA
CBHW050253230526
45470CB00005B/2249